T0380498

Skin Deep

An Interactive Coloring Book

Screebee

African
Americans
Have the richest
Array of skin colors
you could ever see; as
do some other groups too!

Look around.
What do you see?

Every single skin color is individual. There are more than 50,000 shades of brown!

There's Basic Black.
Black is beautiful!
Elegant Ebony. Rich
Mahogany and Regal

Brown. Proud Black. Sun-Kissed Caramel. Dusty Tan. Burnt Sienna. Bubbling Brown Sugar to Butterscotch.

Then there's Sand, and Tan and almost Tan. Hot Sand. Golden Brown. Bronze. Heavenly Ebony. velvet. Clay. Ash. Desert. Dust. Brick-dust! Luscious Chocolate. Rich Sapphire. Sparkling Sapphire. Blush And Rust!

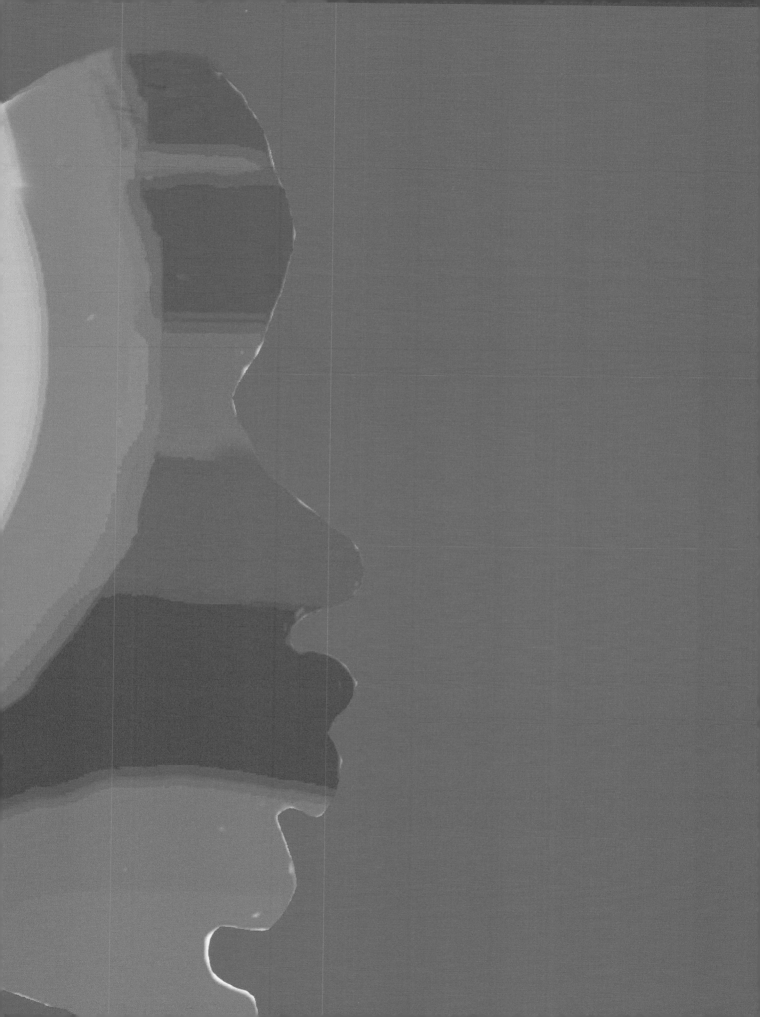

Romantic Black. Exotic Ebony.
Fiery Ebony. Goodness knows.
There are many more shades of
Ebony than one would suppose!
And just as many
tones of Ivory!

There are some clashing colors too, who disagree!

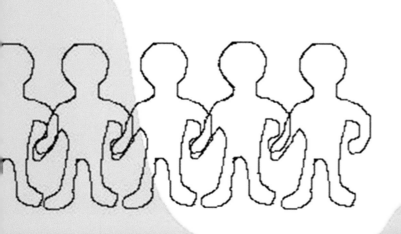

Olive. Terracotta.
Sierra Beige.
Beige?
Yea! Some Black folks
Have even been called
Beige!

African Americans are all kinds
of colors. we're a Royal

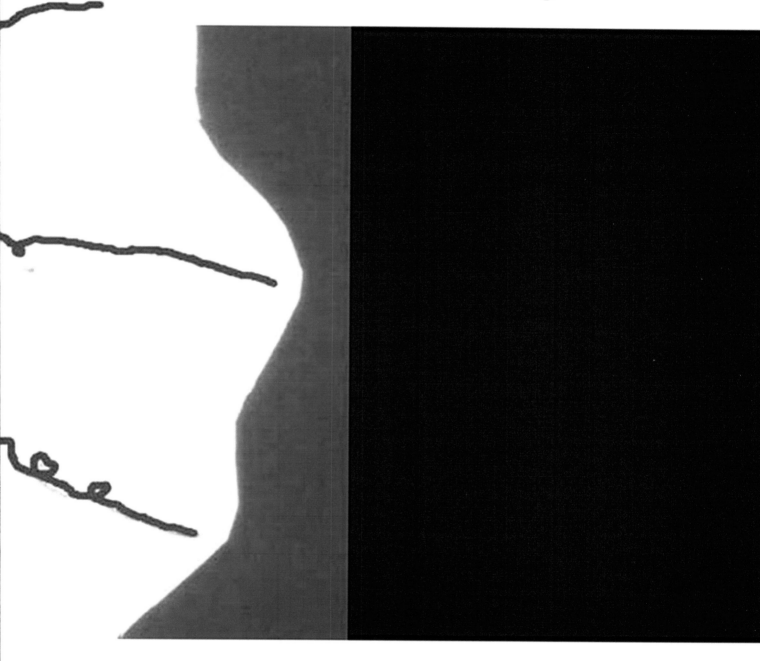

Family of multi-various shades
from Sunset to Sunshine!

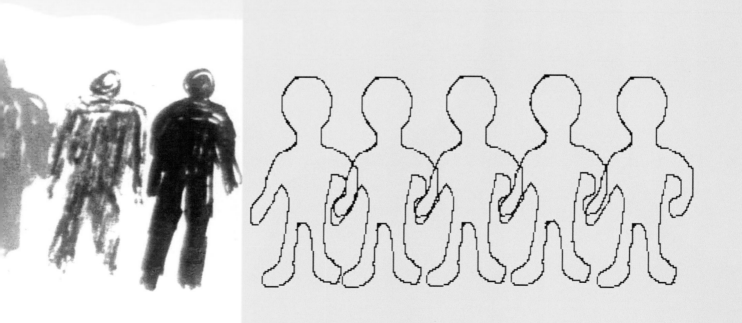

There's Nutmeg.
Ginger. Caramel. Honey.
Honey-yellow—Honey
Brown. Where else can
all these colors be found?

Dark Chocolate. Toffee.
Coffee. Coffee and Cream.
Peaches and Cream.
The most delicious colors
you have ever seen!

There's Burnt Umber. Glazed Bronze. Glazed Gold. Shiny Gold. Cedar. Sequoia. Rosy to Ashy and Rose Clay. Mocha. Negro. Espresso. Red-Bone! Brilliant Brown. Sepia. The Sparkling Coppers and all their many hues too. High Yellow. Almost yellow! Barely yellow to Tarnished Gold.

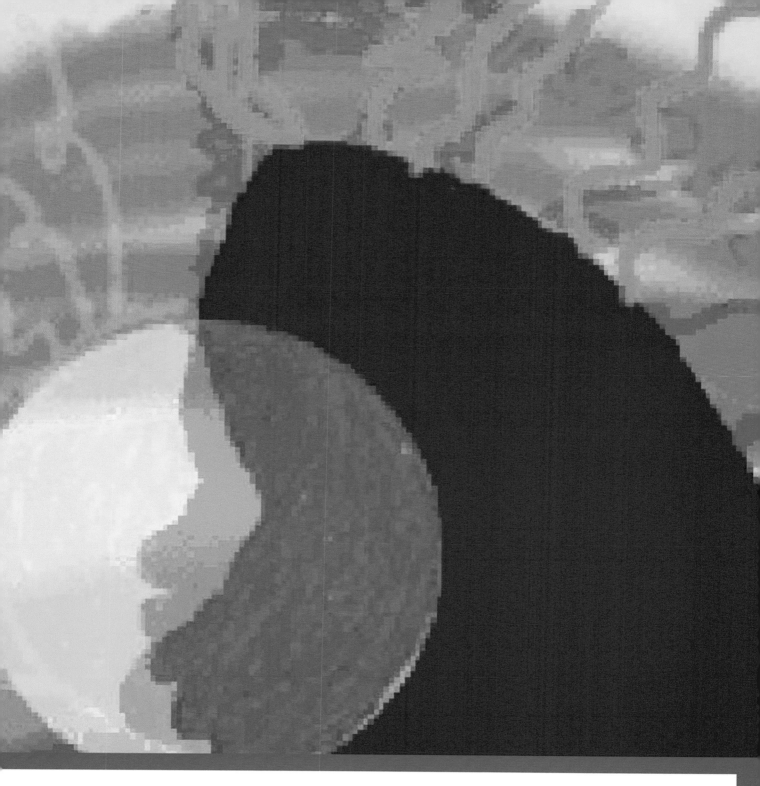

wherever you go proud colors—
from white to midnight,
surround us—like
living rainbows!

Strong—Powerful Black!
Steel Black. Blue Black,
True Blue! Black as Coal.
Blushing Black. Gleaming
Gold. Happy colors and
Clown Browns too,
there's a

kaleidoscope of skin
colored shades and hues!

There's even OREO and
ZEBRA COLOR too!

African Americans are colored
people. People of Color have every

Reds. Hispanic Browns, African Blacks. Caribbean Colored, Asian and white tones too. What a wonderful, beautiful array!

Black is all embracing. That's very precious you see. To this we can add the colors of you and me!

Copyright © 2019 by Screebee. 619909

ISBN: Softcover   978-1-9845-7370-4
        EBook   978-1-9845-7369-8

All rights reserved. No part of this book may
be reproduced or transmitted in any form or by
any means, electronic or mechanical, including
photocopying, recording, or by any information
storage and retrieval system, without permission
in writing from the copyright owner.

Print information available on the last page

Rev. date: 06/03/2019

To order additional copies of this book, contact:
Xlibris
1-888-795-4274
www.Xlibris.com
Orders@Xlibris.com

Printed in the United States
By Bookmasters